A
HOUSE
WAITING
FOR
MUSIC

David
Hernandez

Tupelo Press

First paperback edition, 2003
Library of Congress Control Number: 2002112457
Tupelo Press
PO Box 539, Dorset, Vermont 05251
802.366.8185 • Fax 802.362.1883
editor@tupelopress.org • web www.tupelopress.org

Cover and text designed by Sheila Selden, Peru, Vermont
Cover art background: J.S. Bach "Sonata No. 1 in c minor for Solo Violin"
(facsimile of original manuscript), from the music library of
the Manchester Music Festival.

A
HOUSE
WAITING
FOR
MUSIC

David
Hernandez

FOR

LISA

Contents

I

II

$\mathcal{C}$ontents

III

IV

V

I

Laurel and Hardy Backwards

There was a bedsheet thumbtacked
to a wall, the rattle of the projector,
its one eye glowing behind us like a train

stopped inside a tunnel. In our homemade
theater, Laurel and Hardy were delivering
a piano, pushing it up the longest flight

of stairs. They heaved. They heaved
some more, faces cartooned into struggle.
We've seen this film five, six times.

It's not funny anymore. We waited
until the end, until the filmstrip slapped
and slapped the projector, the bedsheet

radiant with light. Our mother stood
in the doorframe, three months pregnant,
saying it was time for bed. None of us

had seen our lives before—five, six times
or just once. None of us know
about the miscarriage scripted

for tomorrow. My brother flipped the reel,
threaded the film backwards. We watched
a bowler hat leap from the ground

and settle on Hardy's head, slammed doors
opening by themselves. We watched
the two trace their footsteps

and wrestle the piano back down the stairs,
a thing now impossible to deliver
to a house waiting for music.

Mother Limping, Not Limping

Mother limping, with a wire
of pain sparking behind her knee,

with every right step—there,
not there. Mother working in the yard

regardless, working the weeds out
from the earth, heart encumbered

with other work: laundry bulging
the hamper, cabinets and tabletops

furred with dust. Mother yanking
those weeds all afternoon, her body

a machine that only knows dig
and pull, dig and pull. One wrong twist

and her leg ignites, a blue fire,
blue moaning. Mother at the hospital,

sipping anesthesia before drifting off,
before a scalpel opens a scarlet mouth

below her knee, her pulse scribbling
neon grass across a heart monitor.

Mother weeks later, meeting her son
for lunch by the fountain,

underwater pennies flashing
their coppery light. Mother

rolling up her pant leg to unveil
her knee's purple signature,

scar like a notch in the ground
where something furious once grew.

Huntington Botanical Gardens

Boring for a boy: 150 acres
and one hundred times as many plants,
each flouncing its colors. He drags
his bones where his parents want to go.
Here's the Japanese Garden,
a red bridge arcing from green lawn

to green lawn, blood orange carp
fishtailing sluggishly in the pond.
Here's the Subtropical Garden's
fat leaves, blue jacarandas and pink
cape chestnuts. Here's a yawn
blooming on the boy's face,
black petals rimmed with white teeth.

Mother whiffs a rose. Father snaps
a photograph of a peacock
unfurling its emerald feathers.
Too dull for a boy, watching nature
on display like this, flamboyant
and rainbowed like this.

It's all humdrum until the cacti
at the Desert Garden, their million
pinpricks. Walking the narrow
stone path, the boy never felt his skin
this way, so much hazard so close,
the thin hairs on his forearms rising.

A girl scurries by. Her mother
shouts from behind, *Don't run!*

He will remember this. After each
failed relationship and gray silence
that followed, this: the girl's palm
and fingers bristling with needles,
a cactus missing a handful of spines.

Boy Scouts Destroy Dinosaur Tracks

Hands, all the boys needed
were hands, these three boys
in blue shirts and shorts.
And one reservoir below holding
blue water. Three minds
scheming until six little hands
are hoisting the wedges,
sandstone etched with tracks
190 million years old. And the boys
just fifteen, just their hands
as their fingers work their way
under like crowbars, gold scarves
fluttering at their necks. The slabs
lift, break off, calligraphy
of some reptile's ancient lumbering
now in their hands. And now
the easy part, when the boys
deliver the wedges to the sky
and the water swallows it,
blue mouths rippling. What now
and what to do with the boys
clapping dust off their hands?
I say let them go, let their sneakers
emboss zigzags into the earth.
I say the earth will have
the last word, as it always does,
swallowing anything with a heart.
Look: the wind's already
smoothing out the boys' footprints,
sliding its hand over their designs.

Dysfunctional

Under the house the boy
saw the possum, creature
that doesn't know if it wants
to be a rat or a mole. Under
the house where the dark
lies flat on its square back
and the possum's eyes are ruby
in the flashlight's beam.
Playing dead or playing alive,
the boy not knowing which
until days later an olive stench
wafts into the kitchen window.
The boy again under the house,
nose pinched, dragging
the animal by its tail
into the light, into the weeded
yard, marveling how soon
it's greeted by a congregation
of flies. All day—
that's what he has to slingshot
pebbles into the carcass, to watch
the black knots scatter, settle
back on the fur, scatter again.
Until the evening hunkers down
to make the sun its chew toy.
Until father's jalopy
wheezes up the driveway
and mother crushes
a cigarette into her ashtray.
Before things begin to get ugly.

God in a Knot

If God exists in the smallest of creatures

I had Him pinched between
my fingers, had Him tossed

into a spider's web, nature's doily
where He also lived. How fast

His legs moved across the thread.
How fast He became a cannibal,

wings folding up like an umbrella.
Yes, God was the snail suction-cupped

to the side of our house, the snail
we baptized with salt, or placed

on a lit firecracker. Ten, fifteen feet away
and still His amber juices spotted

my brother's T-shirt. And the wasp
I trapped inside a Gerber jar,

that mad buzzing, that hymn I buried
in the yard, in the soil where He also lived,

hundreds of blind deities squirming
under the grass. Even the worm

mother shoveled from her garden was holy:
God in a knot, dead already, snuffed out

by a hand infinitely quicker than mine.

Lice

I hid like this: slinking off
behind the cabinet, bookshelf,
anything in the school library
taller than me. The other students
herded and lined-up, the nurse
dragging a steel comb through
Lori's mane first, then Alan's
bowl-cut. Nothing scuttled there,
or inside Theresa's bale of blond hair.
My face behind a paperback
until someone ratted me out,
someone with shampooed locks
fruiting the air. I scratched
my scalp. The nurse groomed
my dark curls, held the comb
to the window's squared light.
Humiliation makes you wish
you could shrink: doll-size, one inch,
that tiny creature wedged
between the teeth. I waited
for the school bell at day's end,
the shortcut home,
past the tree where bumblebees
tumbled in the grass,
feasting on fallen plums.

Revenge

My brother wants payback
from the boy who lives cattycorner

from our house, his yard carpeted
with weeds, the driveway bruised

by oil stains. The first drops of rain
polka-dot the sidewalk as he crosses

the street, swollen-eyed, fingering
the matchbook inside his pocket.

By the garage door he crouches,
unwraps a piece of the sun in his hands.

I'm too scared to spark my voice
into language, to knock two words

together and yell *Tony, don't!*
I let the wind speak for me

as it swallows the match's flame,
then another. Rain coming down

harder now, but my brother's still
on his knees, still determined

to find a way of dousing a fire
that uses his bones for kindling.

Swimming Pool

Cross-legged we sat at the bottom,
brother and I, a foolish contest

between siblings, our hair swaying
kelp-like in the slow minutes. So long

down there in that concrete room
lit in turquoise light. My lungs

throbbed. A life-preserver glided
across the ceiling. One minute

twenty seconds later and I was done,
pedaled my way up, pedaled

until I was gulping air,
mouthfuls of air, air enough for two.

Beads of water slid off my body,
evaporated on cement, and brother

still at the bottom, serene,
a statue of Buddha in red swim-trunks.

Even when I finished toweling off.
Even when I called his name,

twice. As if it wasn't his name.
As if we could go back to the womb,

breathe fluid again. Dried,
standing at the edge

of the pool's embryonic water,
I waited for his birth.

Exploded View

After a gun is dismantled, the parts
weightless and numbered,
it's hard to believe it's harmful.
The hand spring is a bent
bobby pin, the hammer

a jigsaw piece. Assembled,
when the trigger spring nuzzles
against the trigger, the cylinder slips
into the pistol frame's squared hole,
it's another story.

In third period art class
Jason always drew head-on collisions,
toppled buildings, something
splintering lead, blown apart
with his No. 2. *Very good,*

our teacher would say.
Very nice. That summer
he pressed the barrel to his temple,
squeezed. I floated
through my days, head numb

with booze, forgetting
what I'd just learned: dates,
algebraic equations, the conjugation
of *vivir*—an eraser that swept
across memory's blackboard.

Only the theory of the origin
of the universe stayed with me,
that first explosion, so immense
the stars would always be
hurtling away from us.

Weekend at Ojai

Day one's humidity, the air
saran-wrapping to our skin,
and already the desire to leave,

the lure of highway 33 pulling us
home. That quiet boy
behind the register at the bookstore:

he wants out. You can tell
by the angle of his slouch,
the scar he wears like a bracelet.

Back to our motel room
with its doorstep roach clawing at sky,
its drooling showerhead.

We nap and our bodies float
elsewhere: my wife's in Spain,
I'm at work, wondering why

there's a red mitten in my drawer,
the hand still inside. We awake
at dusk, to a world lit

by a 20 watt bulb. What did we think
we'd find here? And what to do
with what we found?

Have a good day, the boy said,
his sleeve rising just enough.
Outside, a possum waddles across

the shaggy grass, the hedges
quivering where it disappeared.

Two A.M.

Hello full moon. Tonight you're a cracked
dinner plate behind the tree's spiked branches.

Nice to meet you Mr. Panic, and the bowstring
you drag across my nerves. Greetings dark hallway,

bulb-lit bathroom, mirror above the sink
wearing my ruined face. Medicine cabinet,

it's nice to hear you squeak open again,
and the tiny pills rattling in this bottle of Atavan.

I plant one under my tongue and wait
for sedation to lower its warm, green blanket.

There. Now it's time to say goodbye to the moon.
Now the terrors that kept me awake embark:

the lump I found, my wife's test results,
a nephew's eyes slowly rolling towards glaucoma,

and so on—a whole fleet gliding off
into the black waters of the evening.

II

Tempo Records
for Patrick

That record store huddled against the corner
of town held all the treasures a moody boy
ever wanted. Fifteen bucks in his pocket meant
a fifteen minute drive to Tempo, meant greeting
Sara behind the counter with *Hey*, and Sara

replying *Hey*, her hair dyed so black it turned
to blue felt by the window. Nowhere else
would he have found that Pavement EP,
those four songs he memorized like hymns.

Or the Grifters' *One Sock Missing*, blasts
of static from Memphis, damaged melodies
the boy sang in his car, hummed in his room.
In the back, a black door closed and paint-
chipped, bright stickers slapped on haphazardly.

A black door and skinny Jay behind it,
rolling a joint. At the register the boy slid
the Spoon CD toward Sara, pulled out
the crumpled five and ten, two speakers

nailed to the walls of the store thumping
with the sound of Russell Simmons mugging
his drum kit. Sara's eyes bloodshot
from who knows what and the boy's eyes
studying the crisscross of his shoelaces.

Sara wearing despair on her face like blush
and the boy wearing it like a jacket, shoulders
hunched from the weight of it. But the tunes
helped, guitars chainsawing the quiet helped.

And that was six winters ago. That boy
hung up that jacket. That record store emptied
for the Veterinary Clinic that took its place,
for the sick cats, the broken winged parrots,
all those howling dogs waiting for treatment.

Lazarus with Guitar

The overdose turned his skin an aqua-green hue, stopped his breathing...
It was, remarkably, his first death, and only the earliest of many
little deaths that would follow.

—Charles R. Cross, *Heavier than Heaven:*
A Biography of Kurt Cobain

And not until punches
to the solar plexus, the blue
bite of ice water to the face
was he alive, brushing death
from his sloped shoulders,
torn jeans. How breathing
allowed him to pick up
his guitar once more, summon
a riff from its strings, his voice
a blade rasping against the air
until his lips banged shut,
until he splintered his Fender,
raining rosewood.
How opium's black wasp
would find his arm cinched,
vein plump for the stinger, nod
and bliss. Again too much,
again his skin turquoise, heart
stopped. More cold water
and blows to the stomach,
frail body lurching back to us
to screech into another mic,
to strum a guitar bandaged
in duct tape, a song glittered
in feedback. What beautiful
racket you made, what lovely

clamoring until your hands
found a way to quiet
the din inside your skull.
Noise you could live without.
Noise that funneled through
these lyrics, this voice
bleeding from the radio,
resurrected from your throat.

Let's Drink Now

This is where the wrecked convene,
and these the stools they plop
their stories on, the pool table
where they rack their worries
and fool themselves: *I make this,*
the test will come back negative.
Ask the peroxide blond
chalking her cue what's eating her
and she'll look up, expose
the scar zippered shut on her neck
where the surgeon removed
her lymph nodes. She sinks
four, five stripes, takes a long
drag from her cigarette, the smoke
blotting out her face. See that man
hunkered by the jukebox?
He drinks until he's a ship
trapped inside a bottle.
Ask and he'll tell you
it was one dark thing after another:
tunnel, cavern, tunnel, cavern.
Let's drink now. Something
to ignite our embers, heat
for our bones. Round after round
until the floor seesaws,
until the bartender shoves us
into the night and the stars zigzag
over our heads like fireflies
with no idea where to take their light.

Blowing Dust Area

The yellow sign tells it
as it is. Dirt sidewinds across
the highway in curtains,
in waves, ghost of an ocean.

Bundled, a man kneels
by the roadside, head bent
into the grainy assault.
Or a woman kneeling.

It's hard to tell. The desert
keeps rising to drift
where the wind takes it,
hazing everything. Up ahead

it powders the Adult Emporium,
the shop's three Xs marking
where we are: *Here. Maybe
here. No, here.* We squint

at road signs, the dust ticking
against the side of the car
like static. It's this world
reduced to beige monochrome

I'll remember. A tumbleweed
pushed against a chain-link fence.
Whoever was kneeling.
Whatever prayer was asked.

The Butterfly Effect

If a butterfly flapping its wings in Beijing
could cause a hurricane off the coast of Florida,
so could a deck of cards shuffled at a picnic.
So could the clapping hands of a father
watching his son rounding the bases,
the wind sculpting his baggy pants.
So could a woman reading a book of poems,
a tiny current from a turned page
slipping out the open window, nudging
a passing breeze: an insignificant event
that could snowball months later into a monsoon
at a coastal village halfway around the world.
Palm trees bowing on the shore.
Grass huts disintegrating like blown dandelions.

Hard to believe, but when I rewind my life,
starting from a point when my heart
was destroyed, I see the dominoes rising,
how that storm was just a gale weeks earlier,
a gust days before that. Finally I see
where it all began: I say hello to a woman
sitting alone at the bar, a tattoo butterfly
perched on her ankle, ready to wreak havoc.

Wile E. Coyote Attains Nirvana

It is neither by indulging in sensuous cravings and pleasures, nor by
subjecting oneself to painful, unholy and unprofitable
self-torture, one can achieve freedom from suffering and rebirth.

—from *The Four Noble Truths*

No wonder after each plummet
down the canyon, the dust cloud
of smoke after each impact,
he's back again, reborn,
the same desire weighing
inside his brain like an anvil:
catch that bird. Again
with the blueprints, the calculations,
a package from the Acme Co.
of the latest gadgets. Shoes
with springs, shoes with rockets,
but nothing works. Again
the Road Runner escapes,
feathers smearing blue across the air.
Again the hungry coyote
finds himself in death's embrace,
a canon swiveling toward his head,
a boulder's shadow dilating
under his feet. Back
from the afterlife, he meditates
under a sandstone arch
and gets it: craving equals suffering.
The bulb of enlightenment
blazes over his head.
He hears the Road Runner across
the plain: beep-beep. Nothing.
No urge to grab the knife
and fork and run, no saliva
waterfalling from his mouth.
Just another sound in the desert
as if Pavlov's dog forgot
what that bell could do to his body.

Dog with Elizabethan Collar

The contraption looks ridiculous:
a plastic ice cream cone
with a scoop of German Shepard.
Who knows how bad he wants

to paw his left eye, half shut,
twitching in the sunlight?
Once I fractured my ankle,
untwisted a coat hanger to reach

an itch inside the narrow
tunnel of my cast. What joy
that bent wire brought,
what bliss. From the backseat

of his owner's jalopy, the dog
attempts to poke his funneled head
out the open window, rolled
three-quarters down, but the collar

knocks the glass, it clips
the window frame. Poor pooch,
he only wishes to dip his head outside
and feel the kiss of wind.

It brings me back to Jennifer,
cobalt-eyed and apple-scented
Jennifer, how every time I leaned
for her lips, she leaned away.

The traffic light flicks to green.
I press my foot down on the gas
and watch the dog miniaturize
in my rearview mirror

as I steer home to my wife,
my lovely breeze, who sails
into my life again and again
to kiss my lucky head.

The Taxidermist's Wife

All day my husband works
alone in his studio,
works with his dead animals.
Behind his shut door
a hammer coughs, the sound
of pliers clipping something
off, in half. Some days
I only see his back, hunched
over his worktable as he bends
the wing of a barn owl
just so. Some days
only the outline of his body
when he enters the bedroom,
my shadowed husband,
telling me he's almost done
with the grizzly. All night
I feel the great bear standing
at our bedside, paws raised,
paws that once could swipe
trout from a see-through river.
Yes, my hand used to reach
for my husband like that,
his body awakening
in my palm. Now, something
else: my fingers freeze
above his shoulder, stiff
as the blue jay on the mantle
above the fireplace,
the memory of flight
drained from its wings.

The Anonymous

They are playing hide-and-seek with us.
Hunched over their typewriters
in a dark corner, each wears a shadow
that fits them like a tailored suit.

Mid-sentence they'll think of their audience,
the faceless crowd, their voices
silent as one thousand grand pianos
resting at the bottom of the ocean floor.

What we have here is a breed of ghosts,
a piece of chalk moving by itself
across the blackboard, a birdsong
emanating from an empty cage.

What we have here is a reminder
of the secrets we conceal from the world,
each one a prisoner in our psyche,
so vile we dare not utter their names.

Reading Anne Sexton While Eating Watermelon

As I turn the pages of her heavy book,
as I wander through the dark corridors of her veins
where death is licking his bloody fingers

and God is baiting His hooks with hope,
I fork pieces of the red fruit into my mouth.
I descend into the cellar behind her eyes

where Jesus is consoling a lamb
hanging from a meat hook
and swallow another sweet cube.

I savor each poem, each bite of watermelon
until my plate is freckled with seeds:
dead flies on the summit of Anne's skull.

Ropes

I've swung on a tire roped to a branch,
hopped between two ropes arcing in the air.
I've felt the hot orange bite of a rope slithering

out of my fists, loved a girl whose braided hair
was a black rope hanging down her back,
long as the knotted rope of her spine.

And I've helped friends secure mattresses
to their cars with rope, and sensed our bind
slacken when they pulled away from the curb.

But now I'm thinking about the rope lassoed
around my waist, tugging me to the shower.
It's the same rope that drags me to work,

to supermarkets, Laundromats and car mechanics,
dinner parties, gas stations, banks, dentist chairs,
and waiting rooms. A constant wrenching

throughout my days. It's the same rope that falls
from my waist like an unloosened belt
when I am with you, and another rope,

one tethered from my body to yours,
pulls us together, slowly and mercifully.

Grass

Here it is, roadside carpet, the world's fleece.
Jeweled with droplets after a downpour,

yellowed under an August sun. Grown, cut,
shipped to a Hollywood mansion,

rolled flat and tailored to fit around the base
of a marble birdbath. Thai grass,

an entire meadow sashaying in the wind.
Kneecaps lime from kneeling.

One blade yanked and chewed. Grass
where I didn't expect to see grass: a circle

of lawn on a gallery floor, green fringe
sprouting from a crack in the blacktop.

How crossing a field my footsteps flatten
the grass, then vanish in its recoil.

How at the end of it all, when death steers
his mower over my pulse, I'll have to pull

that lush blanket over my body
and sleep under bristling grass.

III

Center Divider

Traffic again, so many cars
crawling south, and I've got
this white block of concrete
to look at, spooling the way it does
by my window, blemished here
and here with a skid,
a crow's wing. I twiddle
the radio dial, every station
glittered with static, so I'm back
at the wall, signatures
left by someone's Goodyear,

and I think of those Chinese artists,
sable brushes wet with ink,
a roll of paper splayed
on the floor, that first mark.
It's the brushstrokes
that tell the subject's outward
and inward qualities, a story
buried inside every swoop,
how gnarled the branches are,
how calm the tree is standing
on a cliff. Same can be said
about these dark stains
rubberstamped along the center

divider, how the subject
is death, its inward quality
fear. Imagine it: you're driving
home late one evening, going
seventy-five, a minivan's taillights
glazing your face red. Then
the hard brake and swerve,
your pulse quickening.

That wall rushing towards you.
That thin barrier between
this world and the next,
so sheer you can see
your hand waving behind it.

IV

Sex and Death

Always the same two themes pushing through
the revolving door of the page or canvas:

O'Keefe's skulls and vaginal irises, petals
engorged and flaming crimson. It's the story

of the teenagers walking their libidos
to a moonlit cemetery, their studded tongues

clinking in the dark. And the mortician,
after a long day of opening cadavers like purses,

comes home to his magazines, glossy women
touching themselves as if to say, *Here I am.*

Here too, how the ashes of a woman I never met
cool inside the urn on a shelf. Gray dust,

bone-chip of pelvis or femur, her daughter
in the next room, *her* pelvis crashing into mine,

the bedroom fertile with the night's soil
for us to plant the blue flowers of our breathing.

Lisa

Last night I traced with my finger
the long scar on my love's stomach
as if I was following a road on a map.
I heard the scream of tires, saw the flash

of chrome, her six-year-old body
a rag doll bleeding at the seams.
It is foolish of me to wish
I was there before it happened, to reach

back thirty years, clasp her small hand
and pull her away from that speeding car
that turned her organs into bruised fruit.
How easily she could have missed

her seventh birthday, the lit candles waiting
for her to blow out their tiny flames.
How easily I could've spent last night
in a crowded bar instead,

my shoulders brushing against strangers,
a man on the jukebox
singing his heart out to a woman
with the prettiest eyes he's ever seen.

Four Days Late, Twenty Minutes Early

Morning rain. Small applause on the car's roof.
We waited outside the drugstore
and watched droplet after droplet swim down
the windshield, their tails wagging like sperm.

I never wanted to be a father, and my love
never a mother. Still, we took turns filling the bowl
of silence with names: *Hannah. Nathaniel. Jacob.*
Isabelle. Through the rain's gauzy curtain

a woman shielding her head with a newspaper
tried the door to the pharmacy. She checked
her wristwatch, disappeared around the corner.
Then a man wearing spectacles tried, his wet hair

molded to his scalp like a newborn's. We waited
until the door gave in. On the drive home
the wiper blades argued with the glass.
We unfolded the instructions from the box.

Three minutes and we knew. Relief, yes,
but also disappointment: two children
playing hide-and-seek so late in the evening
it's impossible to tell one from the other.

Documentary

Elaborate, as far as courting rituals go,
how this bird with satin feathers builds
a stage with twigs, with leaves and moss,

builds it for the one trilling in the treetops.
He flies out, comes back with a navy
feather to weave into his architecture,

flies out, comes back with a blue wrapper,
a blueberry, any knickknack whose color
was born from the sky. This is better

than the news, than knowing the details
of a man who shot his wife, shot her lover,
shot himself: three blood circles that stretched

their diameters into the living room
until I changed the channel. Odd bird,
it flies out again and finds a cemetery

to scavenge, a velvet handkerchief
fluttering from statue to gravestone to wilting
bouquet, useless except for a carnation

two shades lighter than the sea. He comes
back to pin his treasure like a brooch,
back from where the dead are snoozing

under lush grass, and finishes his ritual:
a dance for the one who's finally sailed
down from the trees, dazzled by all that blue.

Crows

Daylight
and I'm given
these scraps of evening

dropped from the sky,
their downward paths
all loops

and twirls, confetti
for a funeral.
One makes a lamppost

his perch, five on a rooftop
like weathervanes,
a dozen or so loitering

on a eucalyptus, ripe
with their raspy caws.
From tree branch

to tree branch they hop
like a bad idea climbing
the rafters of the brain.

Once I held a blade.
Once I was swallowed
by a balcony and stood

too long in the corner
of the night, thinking.
A car backfires.

The branches empty.
Over the ballfield
where a father lobs

a softball to his son,
the sky's holes
move elsewhere.

Cruel

Of course Marcus tethered the lizard
to his remote-controlled Fiat,
drove it up and down and up
the street again, drove its scaly body
raw and bleeding—haven't I told you
about his father yet, his sledgehammer
fists and switchblade tongue?
Who knew what horrors lived
with Frank, a boy with clear eyes
like chipped glass, a boy who blinded
Angela's cat with a firecracker,
a black Persian that lifted
her ruined face to any footstep,
any twig-snap. Who am I kidding?
My parents were angelic—
I could've been cruel to those two
screeching parakeets in our living room,
and I was, banging their cage
when I was alone, lime feathers
fluttering as if on fire. And who knows
what I would've done
to our neighbor's dog if that brick
wall wasn't there. Her barking
punctured the air again and again.
I leaned over the wall and spat, leaned
over and flung dirt clods, bursting
like clay pots on the concrete patio.
If idle hands are the devil's playthings,
he charmed our fingers like snakes,
curled them around this helpless
animal, that defenseless creature.

We didn't stop until our voices
cracked, until acne stippled our skin.
That's when we noticed the girl
next door was a lovely thing
in a summer dress, small hands
lacing up the thin straps of her sandals
as our own hands reached out to her,
pretending they were kind.

Planting the Palms

Wednesday, they begin digging the holes.
Thursday, they kept digging, each man's legs

lost in the ditch of their making, orange vests
vanishing underground after every shovelful.

Nineteen palm trees lie across the vacant lot
until the crane arrives, until one by one

they're lifted. It's sexual how they rise
before the men, their roots caked in dirt.

But now it's Saturday. I've just folded up
the paper, the rape still chilling my skin.

One girl, five men, their zippers unclenching
their teeth. From the window I can see

all nineteen palms stationed along the blacktop,
fronds tied up in green ponytails. I'm amazed

at our hands, what ten could do to a girl.
Only a breeze drifting in from the Pacific,

but still I'm reminded of a hurricane,
of a world dropped into a blender: black wind,

rain falling sideways, a roof unhinged
and flipping end over end like a playing card.

Everything breaking apart except the palms,
an entire row gently bending into prayer.

Suburban Story

When I was sixteen the sky disrobed
her blue dress and slipped into a black negligee.
I unfolded the phone number, called

the married woman who's husband
tattooed her body with his fists. Her dark voice
came through the receiver thick as honey,

moaning *Fuck me.* Moaning *That feels
so goooood,* a necklace of Os
she slowly lowered down her throat.

Downstairs, my parents watched television.
I spilled and spilled, the sitcom's laugh track
audible behind my closed door.

How lonely I was that winter.
The moon was an ornament left behind.
And every morning, before my father

hurried off to work, he kissed
my mother by the kitchen window,
the sunlight varnishing their bodies gold.

Stet

Three times he broke it off
and three times he navigated his body
back to his ex- ex- ex-girlfriend's
welcome mat, her face behind
the mesh screen crocheted
into puzzlement. He didn't know
what he wanted, which way
his heart pointed, a weathervane
slapped side to side by a tornado.
On the porch he stood, nullifying
last week's decision, which nullified
the previous week's decision,
and what a mysterious creature
he appeared to her then, backpedaling
the way he did between indifference
and love. *No,* she said. *I'm sick of this.*
If their tragedy was a comic book
he would've taken whiteout
to her dialogue bubble
and ballpointed *Yes, I forgive you,*
but history's nothing but a transcript
of our habits. The door griped
on its hinges when it closed
while another opened to a landscape
of his making: acres of ash,
black trees adorned with smoke,
the ruin that he was always
prepared to rebuild.

Dissecting the Eye

Ms. Summers, you taught us everything
we needed to know that day you ambled
into class with your swinging hips,
your tin pail and box of razors. Lights off,
the overhead projector overexposed
your face, pale as white marble.
When you outlined the lesson in red
felt-tip, your magnified hand floated
across the movie screen, and what boy
didn't imagine that hand slipping
into his jeans, tugging him toward bliss?
Before we knew it we were rubbing
our eyes in the glare of halogen lights.
You walked up and down the aisles,
bucket sloshing. Yes, before we knew it
a lamb's eye gawked at us from our desks,
a fat pearl onion, gray and glistening.
Some of us were too squeamish.
Some picked up the razor and halved
the eye like a hardboiled egg,
eager to see how it sees: the aperture
of the pupil, the retina's concave wall
where everything's projected upside-down,
where the ceiling becomes the floor,
the floor the ceiling, and you,
Ms. Summers, hung in our eyes like a bat
before something inside our skulls
turned you over, right-side up,
and flipped our hearts, dizzy with lust.

Cheating

It's Sunday when you slant
the shower curtain rod
in place, wedge it between
the tiled walls, silver arm
and its twelve silver bracelets,
its clear plastic drape. Sunday
and a co-worker's wink
on Friday fluttering
in your head, tanned legs
walking through the maze
of cubicles, legs (you can't
help picturing it) now
stepping out of the tub,
glossed in bathwater. Who
could blame your insomnia
that evening, 12 a.m. ticking
toward 1, your wife
purring beside you? Not until
the third hour are you immersed
in the black pool of sleep,
into a dream filtered yellow:
your wife's at a bar,
flirting with a man all smiles
and muscles. You stagger
outside, weepy, and grope
a woman waiting at a bus stop.
You've got a handful of breast
when you're thrown awake,
a clattering in the dark,
your wife calling *What's that,*
what's that? Eyes squint,
you flick on the bathroom lights
and find the shower curtain
rumpled on the linoleum,
the bulged middle
sagging like a parachute
after the long downward spin.

Hit and Run

Midnight arrives hauling its boxcars of hushed minutes.
On the couch you lie awake, eyes sprung open.
From the bedroom your fiancée tosses a *goodnight.*

Outside, the sound of tires rasping against asphalt.
You move toward the balcony, the plum-colored sky.
You see a man by the curb, wobbling, wobbling.

One arm straight and the other skewed.
A black howl builds a nest inside his throat.
The assailant two red dots shrinking down the road.

Police cars, then a firetruck, then an ambulance.
A stretcher unfolds its silvery legs.
The howl takes flight, loops around the block.

You turn away from the evening's freak show.
Back to the couch with your blanket of insomnia.
Your fiancée in the next room, sleeping.

Remembering the first time her lips struck your body.
How you ached the day after, the day after that.
How you anxiously waited for that next collision.

Bones

My parents constructed my skeleton
with coat hangers and plaster of Paris.

While my father twisted and bent
the wires, my mother stirred the bucket

of milky paste with a wooden spoon.
Into the wee hours they built my frame,

bone by bone: the phalanges of my fingers
like chess pieces, the giant butterfly

of my pelvis, the clavicle's crooked stick.
Inside the empty birdcage of my chest

they placed a swinging perch for my heart
where it would trill the only song it knows.

Portrait of Edward James, 1937

painting by René Magritte

Always the panic attack arrived
while doing the mundane.
Peeling potatoes, for instance.
How my mother's body detached itself

like poor Edward before the mirror
looking at the back of his head,
his chocolate curls. Detached
until she hovered behind a woman

peeling potatoes, brown stones
into white stones, the knife
a shard of mirror. Same blouse,
same cropped hairstyle,

this woman bracing herself against
the counter, mimicking a woman
bracing herself against the counter,
half the potatoes still to be skinned,

knife mirroring the kitchen lights,
the faucet's translucent rope
lowering itself into the drain.
Me? My head didn't jackknife

until I was twenty-seven. Night
the world was a carnival mirror.
Night of aerial-views of everything.
My twin, for instance.

Perspective: Madame Recamier of David, 1951

painting by René Magritte

Yes, I understand the feeling. I also obsessed over
death and obsessed over death and obsessed
over death until I turned into a wooden coffin,

my heart a dark knot on the lid. My love rolled me
on a dolly into Dr. Branko's office on a Friday afternoon
and lowered me onto his leather couch. I told him

about the balcony, the edge of the curb, the thoughts
that ruffled their black feathers behind my eyes.
He gave me pills the color of flamingoes, and in one week

my skin softened, my heart was human again. Still,
spirals of wood grain appear on my body like a rash. Still,
when my love and I flatten the space between our bodies

with our bodies, the air is perfumed with pine,
and every splinter she tweezes out from her skin
means: *I love you.* Means: *I'm not okay yet.*

Museum Guard

My condolences to the man dressed
for a funeral, sitting bored
on a gray folding chair, the zero

of his mouth widening in a yawn.
No doubt he's pictured himself inside
a painting or two around his station,

stealing a plump green grape
from the cluster hanging above
the corkscrew locks of Dionysus,

or shooting arrows at rosy-cheeked cherubs
hiding behind a wooly cloud.
With time limping along

like a Bruegel beggar, no doubt
he's even seen himself taking the place
of the one crucified: the black spike

of the minute hand piercing his left palm,
the hour hand penetrating the right,
nailed forever to one spot.

Casino

Bells. Mirrors. So much ringing
and reflection, and now this:
the world's oldest man slumped

in a wheelchair, feeding a quarter
into a slot. Oxygen tubes snake
from his nostrils, an orange canister

balanced on his lap. He pulls the lever
with a hand more bone than flesh.
The machine couldn't care less.

It rolls its three eyes, gives him
one cherry to nibble. Even in this
neon racket his breathing's heard,

clotted and labored, the sound
a needle makes as it skips
on the final groove of a dusty record.

If his life ended now he'd float
through the silver lake
of the mirrored ceiling, through floor

after floor, through the rooftop.
Airborne, he'd see the casino
shrinking below, a twenty-tiered

birthday cake in the middle
of the desert, all its candles blown,
all its wishes still in flames.

Fishing

Cancer's thumbprint appeared
on your mother's mammogram
and your little brother doesn't know yet.
She lets him leave the house

with a clear head and fishing rod.
At the river you watch him bait his hook
and leap from the grassy riverbank
to a boulder jutting from the water

like a large skull. You tell him to be careful.
A hawk glides overhead. Black X
heading east. Your line is first to go taut
and you reel in a rainbow trout with a pink

stripe, a lesion near its unblinking eye.
Your brother poised on the rock, waiting.
You let the fish go. A streak of olive
below the water's glass surface.

Marilyn

Seven a.m., the fog still cobwebbing
the world, and we awaken
to a jackhammer's rattling. One man
drills, another piles the wedges

of concrete into a paint-chipped
wheelbarrow. Beneath the city's skull—
dark earth, a corroded pipe.
Three months since a black cloud

eclipsed your left eye, since they found
lesions on the gray maze
of your brain. Hope is a paper airplane
we toss from a canyon's edge,

our wish somewhere at the other end.
The men keep working,
keep digging around the ruined pipe
until the morning sun burns away

the fog, until the palm trees lift
their veils over their leafy heads,
and the world is visible again,
stumbling forward and beautiful.

Whitman Dying

Walt in the sun, his forehead jeweled
with sweat, the horizon seesawing

until he topples, until he's planted
on a wheelchair. Then another stroke,

another dam erected inside his brain
before Pneumonia steps in,

his lungs two Clydesdale horses
towing the heavy cargo of his breathing.

Then Tuberculosis, his body
giving up now, throwing up its arms,

throwing in the towel. And his heart.
Just look at it: corralled with lesions,

submerged in enough water
to keep tulips purple in their vase.

Now his deathbed, a waterbed,
little waves every time he coughs.

Say your good-byes. Make it quick—
Walt's on a raft, scooting out

into the sea, his beard a white sail
the wind won't leave alone.

St. Mary's Hospital

This one cradles his broken arm and sings to it
a lullaby of moans. This one's all wrinkles and bones,
flopped over an armrest as if put to sleep.
This one gets up even though she says her legs
are numb, two bags filled with sand, and shuffles

toward the receptionist. My body's half ache,
half dizzy, a teaspoon of glass whenever I swallow.
Two hours until the intercom says my name.
I float beside my wife like a balloon tethered
to her wrist, through double-doors and into Room 1.

There's a gurney. I lie across it. The doctor
strolls in with his white coat, his white teeth,
and peers into the sick cave of my mouth.
Tonsillitis, he says. A nurse brings her pinprick,
the antibiotic's blue inferno. An unbeliever,

still I think of Jesus, a handful of mud in his palm
fluttering into wings. How I'd love to see him now,
robe skimming across the tiled floor, hands loaded
with healing. To witness a bone unbreak itself,
the elderly woman jolted back to good health,

her new heart an apple polished against his sleeve.
My throat cured, his touch a necklace I'd wear outside
where the healed are shellacking their bodies
with sunlight, where St. Mary's is vanishing
at the end of the lot, one skyward brick at a time.

Scoliosis

The doctor read my back with two fingers,
read my X-ray against the lightboard,
my spine phantom tracks curving

into the ghost tunnel of my skull.
The problem might cure itself, he said.
Father drove us home from the hospital,

one perfectly vertical thing after another
gliding past the window: lamppost,
telephone pole, lamppost, flagpole.

At the dinner table I sat straight,
coaxing my body to break its habit, to lean
this way. Mother wasn't hungry.

Outside, she pushed sticks into the soft dirt,
tied the rose stems. Surgery, yes,
if my body didn't mend: two metal rods

screwed to my back, a rail where my nerves
carried impulses to and from my brain.
At night, fear rolled up and down,

blowing its tin whistle. Months later
good news. I was ruler-straight,
I was an arrow, and celebrated my body

with a basketball by the side of the house,
the orange Spalding obeying my hands
as I dribbled between my legs,

as I sprinted headlong for the board,
the bloomed roses my mother tended
nodding their velvet heads in the wind.

Life Drawing

The classroom is an aviary of voices
fluttering in and out of coherence.
Someone says something about Goya,
someone else about Parkinson's, the disease

that turns our instructor's right hand
into a pink blur. He walks in, cheerful.
The kimono the model drops to the floor
becomes a bouquet of cherry blossoms.

From my tackle box I pick up a blade
and charcoal pencil, whittle the tip.
I cast a dark line into the empty sheet,
letting my hand see what my eye touches:

waist, hipbone, the sloping ribbon
of the sartorius muscle. Down the calf,
the firmly planted foot, its taut
flexor tendons. Suddenly I'm aware

of my own body, how it works without me
lifting a finger: blood speeding through
the narrow tunnels under my skin,
my heart a ticking metronome,

the brain a computer tall as a skyscraper,
its topmost floors lost in the clouds.
So many bulbs flashing inside
it's a wonder there aren't more glitches.

The model gracefully moves into another pose.
The instructor's hand vibrates at the end
of his sleeve. For two hours I draw and draw.
One miracle after another.

Beginning at the End

A gravedigger unearths your casket,
opens the creaky lid,
and welcomes you to the world
of the living, to the smiling nurse

who escorts you to a convalescent home.
With swollen-knuckled fingers
you sift through the red puzzle pieces
of a farmhouse. Years go by

until you're able to remember
the names of all your children,
until the needles of arthritis
are plucked from your joints.

You rise from your wheelchair,
hobble out the sliding glass doors
and greet your son by his name.
He takes you to your home

where a grandfather clock has its back
against the wall. You meet your spouse
and the two of you witness how time
erodes forgiveness, how the bandage

is lifted to reveal the sore of an affair.
For the next forty years you work,
hand over your diploma like a baton,
then attend college. In high school

you find your virginity, stop drinking,
become a kid. You forget
how to ride a bicycle. You forget
the simple mechanics of placing

one foot in front of the other
and begin to crawl. For nine months
you float inside your mother's womb,
shrink to the size of a comma.

And this is how it all ends:
your life fades away into the shiver
of an orgasm, your parents kiss,
then pull away from each other.

$\mathcal{A}$cknowledgments

Alaska Quarterly Review   "Beginning at the End"

Crab Orchard Review   "Laurel and Hardy Backwards," "Ropes," "Wile E. Coyote Attains Nirvana"

Cream City Review   "Exploded View," "God in a Knot," "The Taxidermist's Wife"

5 AM   "Two A.M."

Green Mountains Review   "Crows"

Indiana Review   "Portrait of Edward James, 1937"

The Ledge   "Bones"

The MacGuffin   "Life Drawing"

Mississippi Review   "Center Divider," "Weekend at Ojai"

New Orleans Review   "St. Mary's Hospital"

The North American Review   "Grass"

Passages North   "Fishing"

Pearl   "Casino," "Cheating," "Cruel," "Dog with Elizabethan Collar," "Marilyn," "Revenge," "Scoliosis"

Poet Lore   "Blowing Dust Area," "Perspective: Madame Recamier of David, 1951"

Poetry Daily (poems.com)   "Portrait of Edward James, 1937"

Poetry International   "Lisa," "Museum Guard," "Reading Anne Sexton While Eating Watermelon"

3³⁵   Gen 2/16 TD

𝒜cknowledgments

Prairie Schooner   "Hit and Run"

Quarterly West   "The Butterfly Effect"

Slope   "Mother Limping, Not Limping,"
                     "Stet"

Southern Poetry Review   "The Anonymous,"
                     "Let's Drink Now"

The Southern Review   "Four Days Late, Twenty Minutes
                     Early," "Sex and Death"

Sycamore Review   "Dysfunctional"

"Wile E. Coyote Attains Nirvana" also appeared in *Verse Daily.*

Some of these poems have also appeared in the following chapbooks:
Man Climbs Out of Manhole (Pearl Editions) and *Donating the Heart*
(Pudding House Publications), winner of the National Looking Glass
Poetry Chapbook Competition.

Special thanks to the Ludwig Vogelstein Foundation for its generous grant.

Many thanks to Marilyn Johnson, Bob Hicok, Denise Duhamel, Ray
Gonzalez, Patrick and Mia Pardo, Ernie Liang, Leelila Strogov and
everyone at Tupelo Press.

Finally, I'm grateful to my parents for their love and continual support,
and my wife Lisa Glatt for filling my life with music.